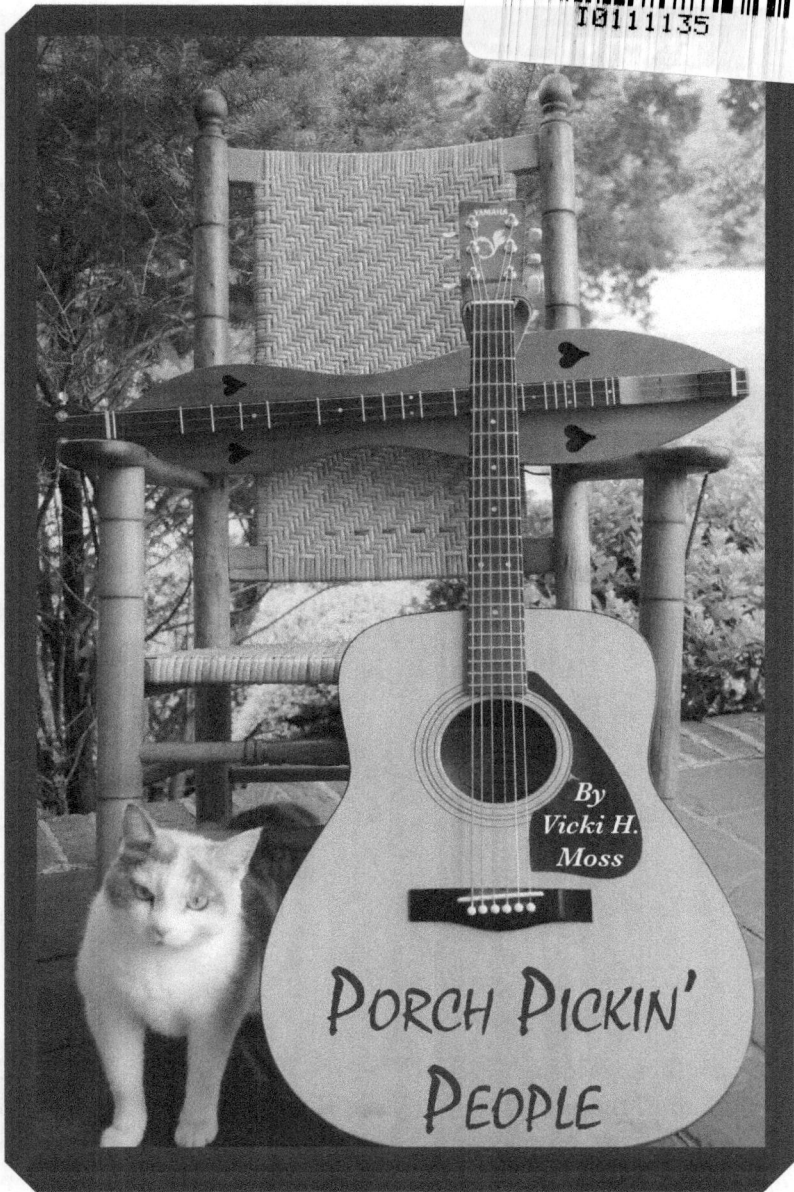

By
Vicki H.
Moss

Porch Pickin'
People

H

Jomága House

Cover photo by Vicki H. Moss

Artwork by Alice Craig

1. Tennessee River 2. Appalachian Poetry 3. Depression Era
4. Malaria 5. Cotton Pickers 6. River Ferries
7. Southern Farming 8. Alabama 9. Tennessee
10. The South

Typeface is Baskerville

Porch Pickin' People

ISBN 978-1-60495-103-5

In memory of Mother and Daddy

and all of my porch pickin' people

and for

the Southern storytelling grandparents

who made my life rich

Acknowledgments

I'd like to thank pencil-drawing artist Alice Craig for incorporating her beautiful artwork into this collection of poetry portraying the South during the 1930's depression era, taking us back to a special place and time of song and survival.

When I had lost hope of locating the right artist to help this book sparkle I decided to go ahead with publication without artwork. Then, I received an unexpected email introducing Alice and I discovered we were planning to attend the same conference.

I needed the perfect artist, and she'd been praying for a broader way to market her work. At the last minute, God connected us. He knows how to bring His children together and, of course, His timing is always perfect.

So, thank you dear heavenly Father, for bringing Alice Craig into my life and work.

Also, grateful acknowledgment is made to the editors of *The Tennessee Magazine* where a shorter version of "The Mighty Tennessee" previously appeared after winning first place in their poetry contest.

Contents

Waiting for Summer Sunday Mornings

Chickens ran across the road at the Ladd's place.
To run them down the women cried, "Boys, we'll help

you catch 'em. As the fairer sex used their dress tails
to keep the feathered friends from running beneath the house

Chollie and fellow yay-hoos caught the squawkers, tied clawing
feet together, hefted them onto blowing horses, and galloped off

leaving women open mouthed, without chicken one.
Free range, free gain. Boys will be boys.

Chickens molted in winter and didn't lay until spring
when they set off. Eggs were marked with a pencil,

circles drawn around the fattest part—never on the ends—
so those could hatch, and the nest robbed of unmarked eggs,

the freshest just-laid eggs taken to the kitchen to eat.
Chicken fryers were cooked in summers for breakfast,

biscuits swimming in hot saw-mill gravy on early Sunday mornings.
No chickens were to be had in winter except for Aunt Willie's.

She, who bore no children but could bear down on a pump organ
in the Methodist church, canned her chickens in jars sealed

until the Sunday preachers' buggies rolled around: Methodist,
Baptist, Presbyterian, Holy Roller, and Hard Shell. Them

pulling their feet at one time or another beneath the table Uncle
Alec cut and assembled, stuffing themselves 'til their eyes bugged,

wiping the grease from wet lips after praise-God grace.
They were lucky to have eggs for baking cakes at Christmas.

Since Santa Claus never could find the Alabama/Tennessee coves
and hollers, oranges and nuts would have to make do

while visions of fried chicken and peach preserves danced
in heads waiting for spring and summer Sunday mornings.

Big Mama's Feather Bed

Big Mama, or Shug, with once-
raven hair now snow white,
raised geese for plucking
feathers to sew bed and pillow
ticking stuffed with down
and feathers that tickled
a nose after a goose pinched
skin. The geese set off thirty
or forty baby chicks that every
now and then when grown, were
robbed of their finery so I could sleep
in that big old feather bed come tawny
summers, sides shushing all around
like sleep hugging clouds
with feathers tickling
a freckled nose too long
in midday's sun…
like sleep hugging
clouds…like sleep
hugging…like
sleep…
like….

Big Papa's Revenge

Big Papa nailed
gray tubs
to the sides
of a barn
languishing
in weed
and wildflowers
for chickens
to nest
and he once
surprised
a chicken
snake curled,
stealing precious
life, apostate
that he was.

Storming home
for his gun
in dust-moted
sunlight
taking life
for life,

eggs streaming
from that big
snake's mouth
meant breakfast
would be cooked
and served
with an egg-less
prayer between bread.

The Mighty Tennessee River

Many things lie
beneath the green
waters of the big
Tennessee—a couple
of black rotting mules
in tattered brown leather
harness that didn't make
it from the ferry
to the muddy shore
with their wagon,
a house that drowned
while a rooster crowed
from its battered
roof, and boats
caught in the suck
dying a swirling death
along with Scot-Irish
longing for forty
acres while holding
on to Revolutionary
War land grants.
Scot-Irish now soggy
in their wet graves.

She used to roll
through the valleys
leaving river bottom
land silted, dark, and rich,
waiting for spring's
next corn crop, but now
she holds to her boundaries,
like a kindergartner
chastised red for coloring
outside the lines, still
holding onto blue secrets
while just passing through.

The Ferry

She was named the Evelyn C
after Chollie's daughter—
the Bridgeport Ferry
that carried people, cars,
horses, and wild-eyed mules
across to the other side
of the Tennessee River.
Painted by the artist Ben
Hampton and hung on the
mountain-home wall, ever
reminding of fear colder
than jelled grease on leftover
morning bacon.

And she terrified me
every time I had to cross
over. Me counting people to
the number of life jackets
painted on the metal box
attached to the side of the
rails, me wondering
who I would try to save

should it be our time
to be sucked down into angry
water, knowing neither parent
could swim. Would they have
traveled a different route over
the bridge if they had known
how horrified I was of meeting
my waterloo from a lapping,
swirling, sucking, dark and cold
snakelike body of water rippling
against the flat bottomed boat
while a tug pushed and shoved,
angry smoke coughed up from a dingy
smokestack whirling into dark gray
skies that threatened to open
with cracks and pealing claps
of thunderous anger issued forth
from a disgruntled God bent
on revenge against an eight-year-old
child who hadn't yet made it down
the aisle for repentance and salvation.
Even if I made it to the other
bank—the metal gate ramp scraping

against the graveled ramp, bumpers
shrieking, grating their way to the top
of the steep egress—would I survive
the trip only to beg never to cross over
ever again, no matter who the ferry's
namesake once was, nor how many
lives the roiling river had claimed,
or the promises of Dairy Freeze ice
cream cones waiting chocolaty cool
and creamy rich on the other side.

I'd rather have eaten chirt rock dirt.

Big Mama's Woodstove

Black, sturdy, solid she
sits waiting for wood
tucked tight inside
four giant round eyes
with newspaper wads
stuffed in between
slivers of rich kindling
hungry for match strike,
round eye lids replaced,
holding prisoner licking
flames kept from escaping,
building, building, building,
until the fire is red hot
enough to fry popping
bacon, sausage, scrambled
eggs, with cooked cat-head
biscuits rising up in her maw.

While bacon and sausage
warms plates in the warming
shelves above, flour is sprinkled
into grease-melt in the seasoned

iron skillet and stirred before
milk is poured to cook and stir,
cook and stir, cook and stir,
salted and peppered then salted
to taste, to cook and stir until gravy
thickens, cooked and stirred,
and Mother calls out, "Ya'll
come and get it!"

Cotton Pickin' Sunsets

He couldn't wait to get away
from the river bottoms, hoe
handles and cotton bolls
that bit beneath tender cuticles
when he wasn't getting bitten
and kicked by stubborn mules
that could kill a man at whim
if the plow and back-breaking
wood chopping didn't kill him
first…along with dirt clods
mingled with chirt rock, clay,
tree stumps ornery
in their never-ending hold
to ever-changing land
that grew silent a few
minutes before gloaming
set in and wild and primitive
critters hollered, echoes
bouncing from across the cove,
mountain to mountain
until a mind not used to

caterwauling sounds
of wild cats, swamp frogs
hootie owls, cicadas,
and katydids with wild
primordial calls of desperation
would make a city slicker cringe
from the violence of nature's
enveloping deep darkness.

A stint in a four-year war
rearranged all boredom.
Toting a rifle during
march miles carrying
a pack with a shovel
and morphine in the event
wounded while exiting
airplanes with a parachute
over lands swarming
with blonde-headed
blue-eyed men searching
to slit country throats
kept a devil in baggy
pants vigilant and alert

surviving stray bullets,
conjured demons, and bone-jarring
landings on full moon nights.

He just thought he'd escaped
from dirt, chirt, and tree
stumps, and angry mules
that hawed, bit, and kicked.
When artillery crashed
around boulders he scrambled
behind while trying to haul
water and medicine to gaunt
soldiers intent on holding
Italian mountains to gain
bitter bloodied ground,
he flinched yet continued
upward to finally set up machine
gun fire to hold Italian turf for allies.

And with blood rivers stanched,
sounds of battle subsided,
anger and loss quieted
for time to fly home, the first
thing he did when he could save

up enough money was to buy
a farm and answer the land's
siren call. But this time, instead
of cantankerous mules with corn
chomping teeth he bought a red
tractor and grew acres gazillions
of honey dew melons, cantaloupe,
watermelons, more watermelons,
and muskmelons while listening to
cows eat and bulls bellow while he
sometimes picked up a hoe to tend
pole-bean garden patches or to detain
a copperhead's heat seeking strike.

And he'd look down into those river
bottoms below—where he'd grown half
tall as Silver Queen corn—hoeing weeds
waiting for unprecedented bounty,
remembering filamental branches of ancients
now long gone with nothing left but dull ache
of precious memory, and he watched
the sun bleed blood red thinking of cold
September ruby evenings and the bite

of prickly bolls waiting for plucking
and it was then he would say to his sweet love,
"Mama, look down into that lonesome valley.
There's another cotton pickin' sunset."

Porch Pickin' People - I

Porch people they were
and sat on the porch
telling tall tales
and derelict lies
about Granny Josie
who once got
the traveling bug
and she and sister
Willie decided to get
off the porch and hop
a train from Alabama
up to Detroit, Michigan
where brother Albert
had latched onto work.
He had his persimmon-
cheeked wife big with child
and children milk drunk
from swollen breasts
and settled in with him,
a musical bunch who sat
out on the front porch pickin'
and singin' like they always

did back home, Southerners
being porch pickin' people
through and through. So Granny
Josie and sister Willie caught
the train on a lark and headed
for the big city. The problem
was, they forgot to take Uncle
Albert's address with them.
he didn't own a phone either,
so they couldn't call for
directions and, "What are we going
to do" they asked each other.
Said Willie, the bossy sister,
"Let's hire a cab and let him
drive around town and maybe
we'll see Albert and some
of the kids out sittin' on
the porch, pickin' and singin'."

"Sounds like a good idea,"
said Josie. So they rented
the cab and had the driver
amble around town several times.
Uncle Albert's oldest son sat

on the front porch pickin'
and singin' until he finally
yelled with a Southern drawl
dripping with sweet tea and butter
from yellow cornbread pone,
"Hey, Paw! I could have sworn
I've been seein' Aunt Josie
and Aunt Willie drive by three
or four times. It's the pea-pickin'est
thing. It looks just like 'em
with flowerdy hats and all."

"Did they ever hold a family reunion?"
another porch pickin' person might ask
before taking a long swig of sugared
tea from a wide-mouth Mason jar.
"Never did. They had to take the next
train back to Alabam!"

Willie loving to tell that story
on Josie while sittin' on the porch
with newspapers spread over flower
dress skirts while breaking pole beans
the color of plump spring grass.

Of course, Josie would just laugh
and say, "It was all Willie's fault,"
and somebody would put a pick to
a guitar string and bend it and go
right back to pickin' and singin'
about tall pines, short legged swine
and God-fearing Alabama porch people.

Porch Pickin' People - II

They were a stoic
people measuring time
by shared crops, fickle
seasons, tree color change,
and slant of light across
summer silk-tasseled corn
fields, who knew the raw ache
of short life by the length
of a pegged nail pine box
laid to rest six feet under
hand-dug ground in a hard cold
rain—porch pickin' people.
They told their struggles
in stories and songs. Sometimes
shielding reddened eyes brimmed
full with pain, they rocked,
reminisced, retiring dog-tired
to light coal-oil lamps while
listening to a fire's embers
tramping snow, as a weathered

gray-bun-wearing woman in a back
room knew first-hand the depths of
agony when losing a child-baby while
helping with an enduring black-night birth.

Pink Slippers

The Lord had never blessed
Aunt Willie with children
of her own though she helped
her sister because she had
a little more than everybody
else without as many hungry
mouths to feed. And when she
came from yan side of the river
to visit sister Josephine every blue
moon, she wore fancy pink
house slippers to delicately traipse
to the community spring house
where everyone kept ice-cold milk,
white round butter, fresh brown
eggs, and yellow cheese—so everybody
could witness her showing off her wealth.

That's When I Knew

The picture hung on the wall—
a tall man named Charlie
in a World War I uniform,
an obvious significant other
surgically removed from
the photo. Asking Grandmother
Mary Kate who'd been cropped,
she pulled another picture
from her closet box of memories.
The same grandfather, but with
an attractive woman wearing
a sophisticated hat, looking
nothing like my precious little
grandmother. "Why did you keep
this picture with Granddaddy's
first wife?" I asked. I'd heard
all about how first wives were
a royal pain for second wives and
were to be systematically avoided—
like the dark plague—at all costs.

"I thought she was pretty
in her fancy hat and satiny clothes,"

came the reply from a woman who'd
never owned a dress so fine,
certainly never anything more than
a printed scarf that kept
the wind from aching her ears
and loose wisps from flying past
a snowy white hair drift.
Shocked to find Granddaddy
had a first wife, I asked, "Well
why did they get a divorce?" looking
for a good reason to be a hater of the
possible floozy woman in the picture—
the jury still out on flooze.

"You're mother never liked her sharing
space either," she replied. "The reason
why she's cut off the picture. But you
see, things were fairly slim-to-nothing
back in those days and the men had
to leave the farms in search of work.
They struck out for Detroit, Michigan.
Your granddaddy had married a bride
loving pretty baubles. He worked at the
Kellogg's Cornflake factory and living
in the big city was right up her alley.

She enjoyed making money that would
spend on life's finer things—big hats
fine dresses. But the whole time your
granddaddy pined away for the shadows
of mountains back home, sounds of a
hunting dog at bay, his voice rising
and dying with the north wind. And tired
of the concrete big city, lonesome heart
yearning for eight inches of deep-plowed
earth over hard asphalt, longing to hear
the call of the whippoorwill flirting
at the forest edge for a mate like a romance
gone bad, he ached for the hoot owl and the
Southern lilting sounds of his kinfolk people
when they sang and danced to the banjo
and fiddle on Saturday nights.

"And she, well, Fancy vowed to stay
and package corn flakes while your
granddaddy elected to come home
and raise crops of corn and kids."

I said, "I guess Granddaddy was hankering
for a lost place, wanting bouncing babies
and a wife not lured by the north star

but enthralled by Orion, the big dipper and blood
moons that enticed gardens of squash, cucumbers,
and okra to grow instead of beautiful bonnets,
enticing factories, and big money."

"Yes, that's about right. And I hope that wherever
the pretty lady is, she's found happiness and all she
ever dreamed of."

That's when I knew Grandmother Mary Kate was a saint.

Searching for Truth in a Different Realm

I didn't know at the time,
being only four years old, that
it was a church where hard-shell
Baptists bent guitar strings
and sang hymns and a preacher man
who couldn't read the first lick,
memorized verses the Saturday
night before as his wife read to him
by a hearth's blazing fire
to cry them out come Sunday
morning like the unleashed
terrors of a thousand pent-up years.

I hadn't had religion beaten into
me nor met the Holy Ghost
that I knew of, and neither
did I understand about the
manifestations of Him while
people were trying to wrap
their arms around Jesus to be
born again by shutting their eyes,
beating their chests, running
through all barriers like a dog

grittin' his teeth traveling
high speed through a silent fence—
trying to get a glimpse of glory
that would stick in one's soul
and pierce the thickest fog of sin.
Later, thank God, my Jesus
used the right amount
of reason and faith
to refute the devil.
But of course I didn't
quite know that then,
so instead I cried like
the baby I was while
most of the women fanned
hot, pasty faces with Popsicle
sticks stapled to funeral home
ads, and my older brother fell
out the unscreened back window
like he'd really seen a Holy Ghost.
Then we offered grace, sang a hymn,
and the amen bench men's words
stuck together on a rising wind
after pronouncing Aaaaaa-men.

Cold March Winds

A cold day in March ushered
stiff winds into the valley
webbed with a thin, tan road
while a seven-month-old
baby with cheeks the color
of pearls lay gasping for breath.
J.C. lay in Mama's arms lifeless,
struggling for air while Daddy
lit out for the ferry across the river
to fetch medicine from the doctor.
When he returned, he was too late,
the baby's cold, clay body already
emptied out of soul and spirit that had
flown.

I remember Mama draped herself across
her feather bed giving over to her grief,
like a wave rising to break over a pristine
beach of whitewashed bones, weeping
like she wished tomorrow would never
come, her heart to the point of a ragged
breaking that could never mend.

A neighbor arrived and helped wash
and clean the tiny frame, dressed him in a fancy
little blue gown, and laid him on the homemade
dresser for viewing. Brother Roy's teacher asked
every classmate to bring yellow buttercups
from dirt swept yards—the only flowers
in February bloom—to punch stems through
a cardboard box lid to place on top
of a homemade coffin notched with love.

Icy wind cut through my thin dress
half covered by a loaned sweater
to ward off the chill and bloody flux.
It rained so hard my next-door neighbor
had to hook his whiskey-drunk daddy's
scrawny team of mules to pull the Model T
from the sucking mud ruts trying to keep us
from the Harris Chapel cemetery
and laying our dead to rest.

Oh, cold, damp-dark ragged grave.

I braced my hand on the tiny coffin
in the back seat between Jo and me
and raised to look through the back

window to watch the boy handling
the harness reins of the mules—I
twelve, he fourteen—and my insides
nearly twisted in two from too much
sadness and gut-wrenching pain, but
from watching the young man…a glimpse
of hope, too. That was the day I fell
in love with your daddy, the day, Darlin,'
I dreamed of more babies one day, and you.

Fork in the Road

The two men worked in the fields,
come sundown sat on the porch
with pregnant wives soon to birth,
and relaxed as the gloaming
crept in. From the edge of
the road a baby bounced in
wearing a white gown with
a deep stitched hem. White
as a ghost, no one said word one,
tongue tied it seemed from
the apparition until someone
said, "Whose baby could that be?"
As the child turned to leave by
another road one of the men
jumped off the porch to give
chase. But the child disappeared
though he beat the bushes
for a trace of substance
before giving in and returning
to his cane-bottomed chair.

No one spoke for quite awhile,
all looking like ghosts themselves.
Until one woman piped out, "It's
an omen. My baby will die and
be carried out the same road
for burial on which the ghost
baby toddled in on."

And true to her words, when time
came for the Lord to take her baby home,
the funeral procession followed the road
up to the churchyard gate, and the other
woman's baby was carried out the other road
of the fork to its own place of rest deep in
the cold, hard earth. And for many moons,
the living sat of an evening, lifeless on the porch,
dreading every cold-coming March wind.

Granny never wept when she told that story about the
loss of her first-born baby girl. Nor did she tell her
husband to curse God and die. She counted her losses,
hanging on to God's promises of a heavenly mansion.

Remembering Charlie

He had a chest like a rock-
breakin' convict's and smelled
of clover mixed with timothy
and red top—a scent that made
her throat ache from swallowed
loving, her eyes sting, and a longing
to go with him as strong as the honking
call of wild geese high veeing South
to warmer climes and a strange land.

He carpentered makeshift benches
and banjos that rang out high lonesome
sounds, and in a hickory-bark-bottomed
chair before hot oak fires, he rocked
colicky babies through the night, this
wide-shouldered stalwart man
that had the sound of mules, hunting,
fiddles, and hound dog tunes burned
into pages of his younger days.
But when his final chapter rolled
around, his black-heathen military
oaths faded along with the tattooed
lady hidden by his work shirt

sleeve along with the winds of youth,
and there seemed to be something
quiet and safe about a gray-haired
fall before the shadowy, tree-filled
dying of winter, as some liked to say.

And she remembered more than
the strain of tortured remembering,
but also enough love that would put heart
in a gray-dead corpse. And she had no
regrets, held on to no grievances, while
cherishing a fruitful life lived on a fragile
cusp weathered by forgiveness.

Home

It was a land filled
with white and purple
sails of dogwood
and redbud in spring,
sweet scent wafting
through honeysuckle
tangles, tulip poplar
blossoms big as cereal
bowls in May as black-
trunked apple trees
blushed to bear fruit.
The Rose of Sharon
bloomed in early summer
with hummingbirds light
as a feather's touch
drinking nectar from
her blossoms, and a woman
had a God's plenty
of lard and flour in
the pantry, and buttermilk
in the spring house

come fall for biscuits
and saw-mill gravy
that floated sausage
chunks the size
of aggie marbles while
steaming next to a patch
of skillet-fried potatoes
and a rasher of bacon
fresh from a just-cut hog
whose hair had been scalded
by water heated over
an outdoor fire, scraped
with a knife when November's
cold settled in before
winter's blankets of snow
warmed sleeping daffodil bulbs
holding onto promises of spring
and her white and purple sails.

The old fireplace where Great Aunt Cleo rocked her babies.

Salt Licks

The salt licks for cattle
had their own troughs
with roofs where cows
or other livestock could stick
their heads inside to lick
up salt to their hearts' content.

Daddy's salt lick wasn't far from
the pond, so after a good lickin'
the cows could get a good dippin'
and a long-coveted drink.

Some say that's why our side
lost the Civil War—lack of salt.
A body can't function without
salt. And when horses and mules
didn't have salt, they couldn't
function properly during war, either.

During that horrendous ruckus
they called civil, people used to
go to the smokehouse and dig
up dirt beneath where salted

hams hung hoping to shake out
some white gold that had dropped
down beneath.

Because gravy is tasteless without salt.

A rebel deserved a little salt in his
bread and gravy, even if his horse
had to do without.

Yet, when building towns in the South
they filled in Mother Nature's salt licks
with clay and soil so they could lay asphalt roads
and concrete sidewalks—places covered
over where the wildlife used to come for
their salt. And salt blocks were manufactured
for livestock—easily hauled home in the back
of a pickup.

But where do the deer, coyotes, and other wild
animals find their salt now? Are ants enough?

Stoicism Personified

She killed the car engine
by Great-grandmother's
grave knowing her story
ran like a river of sadness
through a valley where
loving was sometimes bereft
of vows and only tendered
with false hope and empty
promises. Five children,
losing a husband, and with
one on the way fathered
by a man with a mercurial
heart and no lingering looks,
who plowed more fields
than he could support
in a time when times
were hard, money scarce,
and a barrel of ice cold
crunchy kraut sittin' on
the back porch had to
stretch a month of Sundays.

She left that valley to strike
out on her own like a wandering
Rahab relying on God and a prayer
to help feed hungry mouths
and the wood's filly born
who would find more
love than her mama
ever had—a child
with a daddy who
never acknowledged
her name much less her
sweet face. He missed
out on a jewel—wonder
if he ever hung his dark
head in shame?

Wonder if his
lips ever formed her name?
Wonder if in his sleep
he ever dreamed about rubies?

Healthy Eating

I saw that petite
woman march out
the back door
catch that free
range Dominecker,
wring its neck
with a murdering
hand intent
on killing,
while a hatchet
lay on a tree stump
chop block within easy
reach no less
impressive than
the double axe
waiting for Ann Bolyn.
Was her only crime
not laying enough eggs?
I watched as the addled
victim stared into
a cloudless azure sky—
beady eyes filled

with fright, feathered
friend lips moving
as though breathing
a Holy Jesus prayer—
and wondered if anything
traumatized could be healthy
eating. Until then
I'd always thought
chicken legs walked
out of the freezer section.

Dog Days Were Over

I'd never heard
him raise his voice
until his precious
Penny was shot.
But that night
a hush fell
over the house
as children clamored
to get out of his
way so he could carry
his blood-dripping pet
inside, kids peeking
around door jambs
to glimpse the fallen
comrade.

Penny survived by way
of his best friend
nursing him back
to health, pushing
jelled Tony's dog
food from a spoon
with a thumb

between grinning
lips that only
fooled kids into
thinking he was happy.

When his friend passed
away, he didn't last
long either because
no one else was going
to spoon feed a man's
dog who hiked a leg
on peonies and scratched
in the dirt to uncover
tulips and iris, intent
on beautifying God's
creation—especially
when there was chicken
to fry for funerals,
the sick to visit,
church to attend,
peaches to can,
Wandering Jew to water,
and flowers to deadhead.
Dog days were over.

The Grownup Table

No kids allowed
at the grownup
table, its rich
dark legs reaching
out like tree roots
embedded in the floor,
its table top covered
with lace held down
by a spread of turkey,
green beans, mashed
potatoes, sweet potato
casserole with brown
sugar oozing hot butter,
sage dressing, rolls,
sweet tea, jelled cranberry
sauce, Dr. Pepper cake,
pumpkin pie, while long
legs mingled beneath
and longer faces waited
out prayers when I peeked
to see if grownups opened
their eyes during Jesus
talk.

And I can't wait to sit
at the grownup table I
thought, but then I didn't
realize the privilege came
with a price—big bellies.

That Ol' Heifer

That ol' heifer
birthed a new calf
and stayed locked
up in the barn lot.
Don't go in.
That ol' heifer
she'll get you down;
she's mean as they
come, that ol' heifer.

That ol' heifer
would chase
a body down;
didn't have
a lick of sense.
Stay away
from that ol'
heifer now. She'll
get you down.
Now stay away,
I say. Stay
clean away.

But Evelyn didn't
want to go around
that ol' heifer.
She'd take a short
cut any time through
the pasture. Didn't
have a blame lick
of sense looking
all around,
that ol' heifer
charging higher
ground as she ran
to the fence.
Not near as fast
as she thought
she was, that ol'
heifer gaining
ground. She'd
never make the
fence but for saving
grace. That ol' heifer
slipped on slick ground
and gave a chance

to that ol' heifer
who learned her
lesson.—Don't go
dallying around no
big ol' heifers.

Hog Killin'

Following those
headed to the hog
lot, rifle in tow,
we climbed on
top of the fence
being warned not
to fall because
a mad hog is a bad
hog…Will eat you alive
hog…Don't you know
hog…as the rifle aimed
steady and true
and a crack filled
my ears as a sad hog
took a bullet between
the eyes. Seemed
awful how the dead
carcass was boiled
in a tub lit by
burning fire scalding
hide and hair before

scraped clean with
knives sharpened
thin to do their
dirty deed stripping
a corpse naked.
And I watched them
hang that lump of swine
by chain and open
his belly for all
to see and as its
innards fell
to the ground
slick and round

I was glad that 'ol hog wasn't me.

Let Me Get the Crop Out

They told stories
about people of old
in Sequatchie County
where a person could buy
off the law for five
hundred dollars, and how
Junior was jealous
of Clem and held him
down in the river playing
the ducking game,
dragging him to shore
though he couldn't
resuscitate him—but he
was down one less man
flirting with his wife.
Maybe he was tired
of her saying, "Go
home with me, we'll
have some blame fun."

They lived in places
called South Coon

Creek, Island Creek,
Hog Jaw Valley,
and every now and then
somebody got hold
of some bad whiskey
and cut the heads
off two of his friends,
called the law
and got out of it
'cause you could buy
the law, remember?
How you could buy
the law?

It was a time when
if you threatened
a man you could
join the Army
or leave the state
by raft down the river
to a new place
and land at
the mouth of another
river to start life

all over again
in another cove.
By Jove, the law
wouldn't hound
you in another cove.

And it was a place
where women barely
tolerated drinking
men who flicked
yellow jackets
from off their
pot of steaming
corn mash
while children
choked back
worms crawling
heaven bound
to find daylight.
And one Mother
Mary said to her man,

"If you
don't quit
your drinking,
by gum I'm
gonna leave you."
And Jim Andy
said, "Wait
'til I get
the crop out
and I'll go
with you."

Tornado Alley

The trees shook
from violent winds
that blew through
electrifying land
that supplied
daily corn pone
and buttermilk
from cows that lay
low with a knowing
that a mighty storm
was passing through
while gentle folk
hunkered down in
rickety tin-roofed
shacks wall papered
with last year's Sunday's
news to keep the snow
from blowing through
the thin mud chinks.

And when silence fell
like death all around, those
left living climbed
those newsprint-covered
walls that had collapsed
around them, never taking
time to read about the latest
wood stove's arrival at the local
hardware store, feeling
like the hand of God
had waved over their hallowed
piece of ground.

The Almighty Dollar

It was a time when
a rifle could be left
over the mantel with
a door unlocked
and nobody stole,
even though you
might come home
and have somebody
listening to your
records circling the
phonograph.

And he said, "I hauled
coal off Whitwell mountain
to North Chattanooga
for fifty-cents a load
with a truck driver named
Mr. Terry, him letting
me drive it up as the old
man drove it down twice
a day. Loaded it. Scooped
it. Made more money

in the Army than
when I came out.

And Charlie used to
be part owner of the
South Pittsburg ferry
with Uncle Albert Terry,
and sold out to Albert
when one day afterwards,
Albert pulled out a roll
of bills that would
choke a cow and said,
'Chollie, half of that
could have been yourn
if you'd just stayed
with me.' Always
had an eye on how
a dollar could be
made to put food
in kids' bellies
and clothes on
their backs once
the cotton crop

was in. Everything
depended on the
almighty dollar
and pocket change.

Nothing's changed.

Sleeping with the Hogs

Frank Guess
lived at the head
of Hembree's Cove
in a house propped
on stone piles
with a kettle pot boiling
from a hot fire,
and the hogs
would raise
the house off its
foundation of a night
to where a body couldn't
sleep. So ol' Frank
liked to sneak down
there with a boiling
pot of water and throw
it on the grunters
and squealers;
then he'd laugh
"HA HA HA HA"
for a week.
He'd rather laugh
'fore he'd eat or sleep.

Forty Cents on the Dollar

Uncle Alec hated
a black crow
worse than
bone dry seasons
without warm summer
rain, and he'd pay
twenty-five cents
from a dollar
to the boy who
could keep the devils
from eating
up his corn. So
a smart boy knew
he could kill two
crows with a shotgun
and one crow with
a rifle, but shotgun
shells cost five
cents a piece.
So he did the math
figuring he could
make a dummy crow

by taking black
plastic, wrapping
it around a coat
hanger and throwing
it down on the ground
to lure the evil
destroyers in screaming
their "caw, caw, caw."
Then he'd make sure
to line up two shiny
dark demons in his
sights and take home
forty cents from a dollar.

Those country boys
could take a forked
stick for stock
and cut strips from
tire inner tube
and shoot sycamore
balls out of a tree
using the tongue of
a shoe, so it's no
wonder they fought

and won the war
across the Big Pond.

Back when you could
make forty cents on
a dollar.

Come Spring

Come spring Mark
liked to smell
eight inches under
and he'd say, "Know
where I can get a garden
tiller?"

He'd plant
potatoes in February
in a six-inch deep hill
with dirt over it; radishes,
lettuce, green onions, corn,
okra on the twenty-fifth
of April; green beans
on Good Friday, claiming
they'd do better; tomatoes
on the twenty-sixth
of May when all sign of
frost was gone or he'd
put a milk jug over
the plants. Then he'd
plant shucky beans and pole

beans later, gather cane
on the river bank and stick
'em when the runners started
coming up, making a tee-pee,
and tie them at the top when
they came up in two rows
one hundred feet long.

At six a.m. he'd milk,
at five p.m. he'd pull teats
again. When the cows would eat
wild onions he'd allow it to be
churned for buttermilk and butter.

Then he'd go gather poke salat
in the woods and wash it three
times (so it wouldn't piezen him)
before "frying it in grease with
an egg to give my bowels a good
workin' out."

Had It to Do

On a day when humidity
and heat could rile the dust,
when copperheads crawled,
rattlesnakes rattled, and fat
cotton mouths plopped from
dark tree limbs into a man's
fishing boat while he was trying
to do nothing more than pull
bream and crappy in on a hot
August day, a wise man elected
to go swimming.

It was a place where Barney Cagle
was throwing down lime and was hit
by a rattlesnake, and once Billy
Stokes was two-fanged by one and his
leg 'bout rotted off, and when George
Cooper's hand was struck by a copperhead
he turned up a pint of whiskey and never
went to the doctor cause he knew holler
moonshine would thin venomed blood
or cause him not to care if his leg
rotted off or not.

It was a place where Earl Ragin's
dog was shot with a double barrel
shotgun for messing around the barn
where the shoats were kept. It was just
that kind of place and a man orta learn
to keep his dogs at home.

So when Ellis Colvin kept rowing
people across the river, cutting into
Jim Cooper's income from his river
boat service on a day when
the humidity and heat could
rile the dust fast as tempers,
Jim pulled his gun and shot
Ellis down like he would a
snake or a low lyin' dog
creepin' up on unsuspecting piglets.
He then punctuated his act
by removing his hat, scratching
his head, and adding, "I had it to do."

Alice Craig

Maude

Give Maude some trauma
and she'll add it to her
memory bank. She's easier
to keep than a hoss. Her
feet stay in better shape
than a hoss and when the
branches of the oaks
quarrel like a houseful
of kids on a rainy day,
she won't jump from beneath
you like a buggabear's
'bout to eat her alive.

She'll rarely go lame
and won't founder herself
to death like a hoss,
though like the mule she is
she may kick you
every now and then.
But mind you she
will eat concrete

if you leave any bags
layin' around and you'll
have to give her a dose
of castor oil to keep
her bowels from locking up.

But that's just Maude.

Fixin' Nuthin'

Gordon Hembree lived in
a two-story white house with
a blacksmith shop, and Albert
used to go there with his daddy
to turn the blower while Grover
took a look at a mule's foot,
sized it up with a good eye, then
shod his mules. When Maude
would lay down on Grover's bent
back he'd whop her with a rasp
to the belly and say, "Get
off me!"

Once when Albert warped
the mules with the line
and broke the plow point
on a rock Grover said, "Boy,
you can tear up hell and fix nuthin.' "

666 Tonic

Back in the day
Albert plowed one day
and chilled the next.
When plowing, he'd go
a half mile to the end
of the field and let
Maude rest in the shade
while he picked up a hoe
and helped sister Aileen
weed while fighting off mosquitoes.
Next day he'd drink 666 Tonic
to fight bone-racking chills.

Tennessee Valley Authority
provided screens and wood
for the doors to keep mosquitos
out, but there were no screens
for windows or three inch
cracks in the walls. Plowin'
folk sweated all week, took

a bath on Saturday night whether
they needed one or not, hoping
to ease the bite of long hard
Monday through Friday rows.
A bath once a week was better
than twice a year since that was
all their ancestors ever had 'cause
bathing was considered unhealthy
back in the old countries.

Come Monday, he took up
the plow lines and gee'd
and haw'd his derelict-looking
mule all over again until
it was time to drink 666 again.

Either day, come Monday,
he had his row to hoe.
Same as the devil.

Church Meetins'

Albert didn't know much
about church growing up,
only what his mother and
grandfather Noah read to him.
But he always used to volunteer
to take the other young folks
to church meetin' in his wagon.

He didn't darken the doors, but
held to his excuse he had to stay
with Maude and Mandy; plus he
knew there'd be hell to pay if
something happened to his daddy's
prized mules.

When he stayed with his Uncle Alec
and Aunt Willie to help get the crop
out one year, he attended on Sundays,
but his mind was always on yan side
of the river where he knew his buddies
were playing ball.

What finally got his attention to make
his heathen self call on God was when
flying over the Atlantic Ocean after WWII
and he could see the white caps not that
far below due to a moonlit night.

"What a shame to live through a World War
jumping behind enemy lines to fight my way
out, to die by drowning if a submarine captain
who hadn't heard the war was over took a pot
shot at us and our plane went down. I never
learned how to swim and was afraid of drowning.

"That's when I called on God. 'Lord, if you'll
let me live, I'll stop drinking and gambling and
go home and settle down and start a family.'

"The Lord heard. And here you are little girl.
I was good with two, but the Lord also gave me you."

Green with Envy

Grandmother said her friend
lived her mountain childhood
never knowing, but always
wishing her father would
come riding in on a white
shining horse to carry
her off to be his precious
little princess.

When she was grown she sent
him a letter addressed to Johnny
and it read, "My momma says....
I just need to know if you're
my father. We don't
want anything you have
— we probably have more
than you do. Just please
tell me, are you my daddy?"

He ignored the letter and she
stopped dreaming about knights
on white horses or about being

a pink-ball-gowned princess
and her horse turned jaded.
Instead as she picked yellow
neck squash and blood red
tomatoes from a copper colored
snake- infested garden, growing
green with envy of the other girls
with mule-plowing overalled dads.

Saddest story I ever heard.

When Long Whips Cracked

They came from a time when
lye soap took hide and all,
and if it didn't turn out right
when made, then witches riding
brooms had bothered it; and if cows
gave bloody milk they'd
been bewitched as well.

They came from a time
when humans took birdbaths,
preachers exhorted, and winners
who fought enough flapped
their arms and crowed from a stump.

They came from a time when
pistol shots rang out, long whips cracked,
whiskey was dry-throated through
the mail, and believing if a pregnant
woman jumped over barbed wire
it would make her baby hair-lipped.

They came from a time when heads bowed

on Sundays, spirits broken and hearts full

of remorse, they vowed their vows to God

and held onto their blue-thin dreams

while petitioning their Savior to bind

the malaria from taking them down

to sheol. And what a time it was.

Belly-Empty and Biscuit-Bread Lean

The man-person he'd become
had seen enough killin' so
he packed up his rifle-gun
and left a-warrin' all his days.

Traveling home to the piney-woods
he took some flower-thingys,
found a girl who would be his
mother-woman and took her
to a preacherman on a ridin' critter
and they sang a chanty song
the entire Blue Ridge way.

They had times of being belly-empty
when biscuit bread was lean,
and the cow-brute gave onion
milk, and the granny-woman
trudged a mile to help relieve
a tempest storm of pain.

And when the hunter's moon hung
bowl-full in the ink-dark sky
slung-low shining down-log
they said, "As long as we be God's
children, we'uns have everything."

The Circuit Rider

Sheepskin held a circuit rider's profession that appeared
to call for a seamed leathery face. He took a vow of poverty
but was rich in the faith, easy to spot in short black breeches,

double-breasted black coat, long stockings, and hair parted
in the middle and draped to the shoulders like a temple veil
to accentuate the sanctified look while he road hymnal-like

through mist that hung over dripping mountains shagged
with ancient hemlock. Unmarried, uneducated, zealous,
and young, he traveled back roads zorting on turning

out wayward members for dishonesty, lying, stealing,
communing with other denominations, holding to erroneous
doctrine, and fornicating. He discipled on clearing the rolls

of those who fought, drank excessively, gambled or played
cards, or had an unhealthy interest in their neighbor's wife.
And when he left the tavern stump for the next holler, he

accepted the pint of whiskey with grace to help fire up
his spirit for the next group of Sunday-Breaking Sabbath-
Desecrating sheep who had become indifferent to the Master.

He was a good hater ordained with powerful resentments
and partisan zeal, who rode through snow and ice on days
when offering redemption through Jesus while wearing

holy long john's—though not by religion—on days where
nothing was out but cackling crows and Methodist Preachers
ridin' horse critters that needed a good graining and relief

from a bad case of hoof thrush. And sometimes, like the Hebrews
rythmically marching around Jericho to create
a resonating effect that brought down the walls, he circled

his lonesome campfire quoting Othello—the only Shakespeare man
he knew— "It is the very error of the moon; she comes more near
the earth than she was wont, and makes men mad."

For he was from deep-water ancestors sometimes longing
for home, other times waiting out an angry rain searching
for a downhill creek, declaring to have found the Living Water,

proclaiming faith is all we have, see it through just like snow
eventually finding a river while smoke mingles
over a misty haze.

A Hound That Don't Lie

A stanch dog is loyal, steady, and true even
though he may be a cur of questionable
lineage. Keep your hunting dogs penned;
nobody wants an egg-sucking back tracker.
Go to first Monday at the Courthouse and get
you a rangy hound to run deer and wild hog,

a bandy-legged beagle to chase swamp rabbits
and cottontails. And an elegant pointer with a
bend in the back legs as a sign of rugged strength

will keep you in pursuit of dove until you know
there has to be a dog heaven. And the eyes—
don't forget the eyes. True character of a dog

is often seen in large clear eyes that make
you want to melt right down into them. That's
where you'll see the character of a hound.

Same as a man.

A good dog is one hound that don't lie.

Same as a man.

About the Author

Vicki H. Moss was previously a pundit for the *American Daily Herald*, Editor-at-Large and Contributing Editor for *Southern Writers Magazine*. A poet, blogger, speaker, free-lance editor, ghost writer, Vicki is frequently on faculty as a workshop instructor along with school author visits. Author of *How to Write for Kids' Magazines while working on a debut novel*, *Writing with Voice*, *Nailed It*, *Adrift*, *Smelling Stinkweed*, *Rogue Hearts*, and *Roisin Dubh*—a poetry chapbook, she always has a work in progress. Writing for many venues, she's published over 850 articles and poems in Scotland's *Thistle Blower*, *Country Woman*, *Christian Devotions*, *In the City*, *Hopscotch*, *Boys' Quest*, *Southern Writers Magazine*, and Cecil Murphey's book *I Believe in Heaven*. She's written over forty stories for the *Divine Moments* series published by Grace Publishing. Follow her at LivingWaterFiction.com and follow along on Instagram @vickihmoss, Twitter @ VickiMoss and Facebook.

About the Artist

Since the age of 3½, Alice R. Craig has been drawing. After the loss of her child in 1996, she felt God leading her to use her artistic skills in ministering to others who have lost infants and young children. Focusing more on God's calling to ministry, her artwork and sketches portray hope and encouragement in the midst of trials and hardships, and if so desired can be personalized. Alice is now using her drawings and speaking gift to touch the hearts of women across the nation. She can be contacted through her web site—*Artistic Memories by Alice Craig*—at www.aliceart.net.

www.ingramcontent.com/pod-product-compliance
Lightning Source LLC
LaVergne TN
LVHW021409080426
835508LV00020B/2510